FAVORITE POP PIANO SOLOS
27 HITS, STANDARDS & THEMES

ISBN 978-1-4234-1852-4

HAL•LEONARD®
CORPORATION
7777 W. BLUEMOUND RD. P.O. BOX 13819 MILWAUKEE, WI 53213

Visit Hal Leonard Online at
www.halleonard.com

CONTENTS

ALL I ASK OF YOU
from THE PHANTOM OF THE OPERA

Music by ANDREW LLOYD WEBBER
Lyrics by CHARLES HART
Additional Lyrics by RICHARD STILGOE

AUTUMN LEAVES

English Lyric by JOHNNY MERCER
French Lyric by JACQUES PREVERT
Music by JOSEPH KOSMA

Slowly, with longing

BALLADE POUR ADELINE

By PAUL DE SENNEVILLE

Slowly

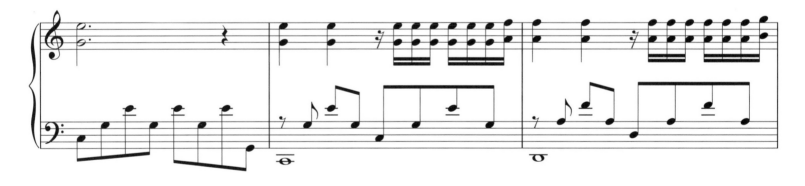

BELLA'S LULLABY
from the Summit Entertainment film TWILIGHT

Composed by CARTER BURWELL

Moderately

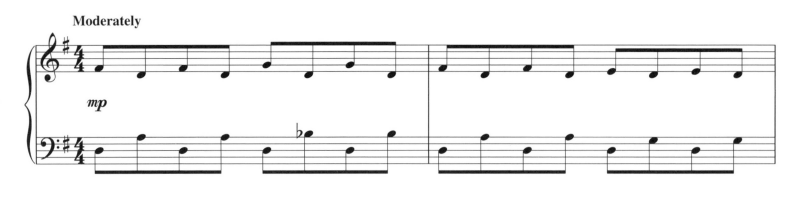

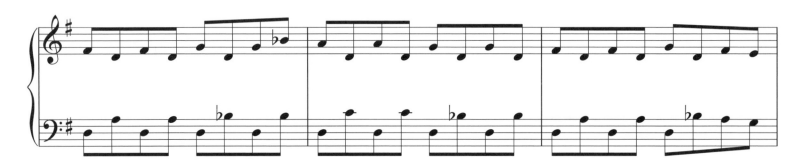

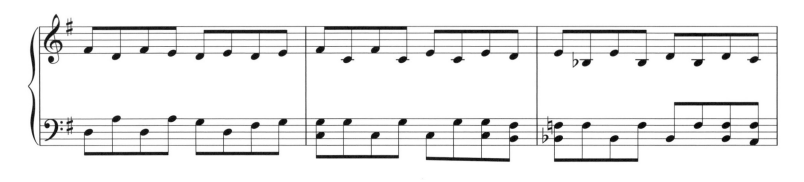

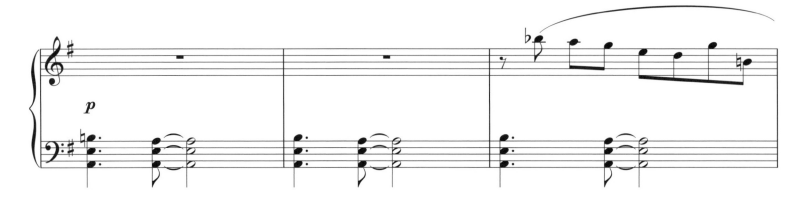

BOHEMIAN RHAPSODY

Words and Music by
FREDDIE MERCURY

CAVATINA
from the Universal Pictures and EMI Films Presentation THE DEER HUNTER

By STANLEY MYERS

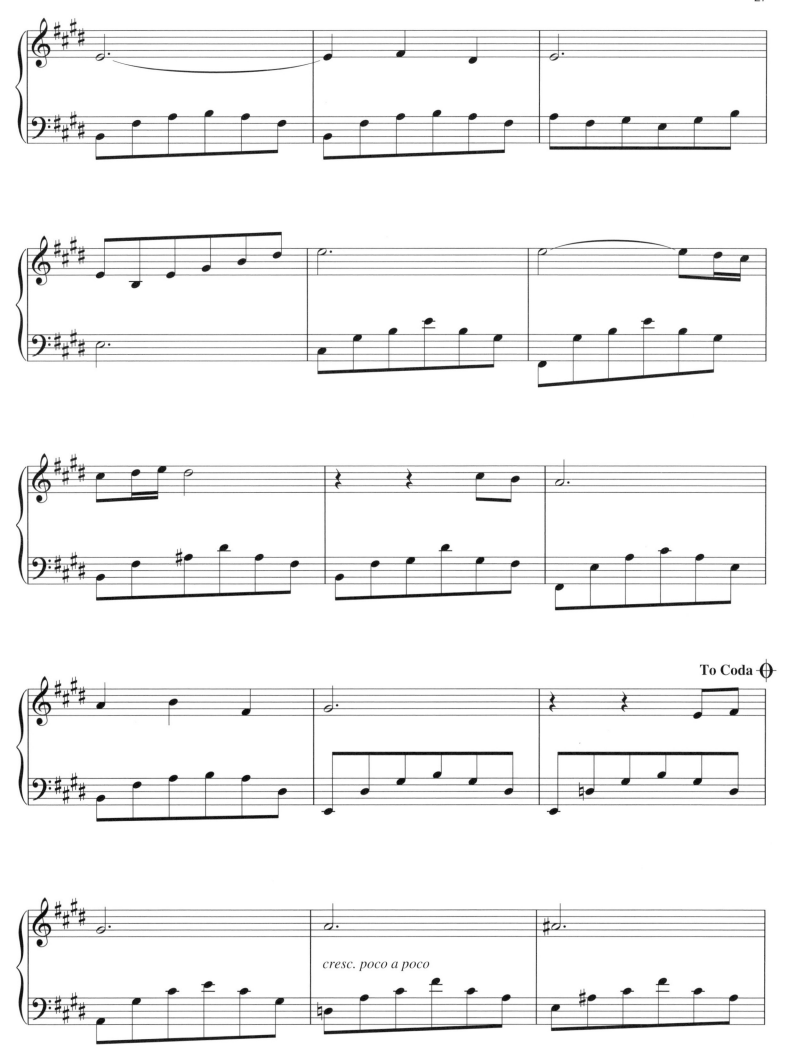

To Coda ⊕

cresc. poco a poco

D.C. al Coda

CODA

poco rit.

molto rit.

DON'T STOP BELIEVIN'

Words and Music by STEVE PERRY,
NEAL SCHON and JONATHAN CAIN

D.S. (with repeat) al Coda

CODA

Play 3 times

rit.

FIELDS OF GOLD

Music and Lyrics by
STING

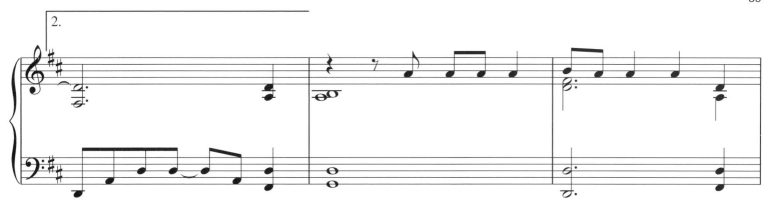

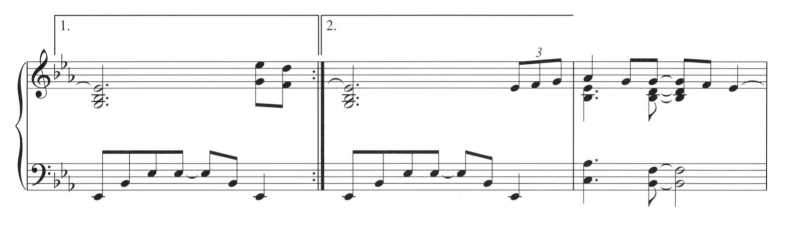

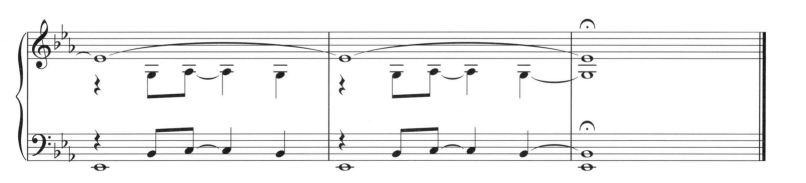

FORREST GUMP – MAIN TITLE
(Feather Theme)
from the Paramount Motion Picture FORREST GUMP

Music by ALAN SILVESTRI

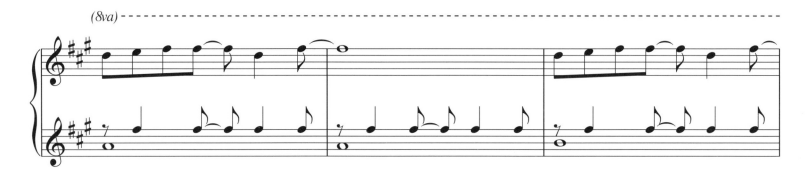

(lightly)

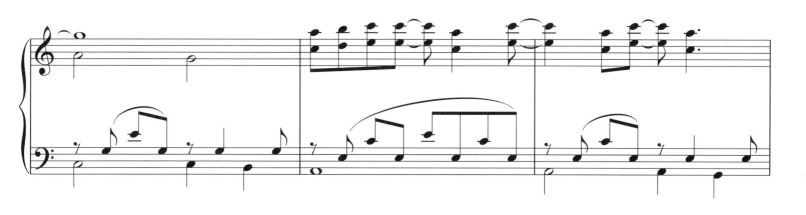

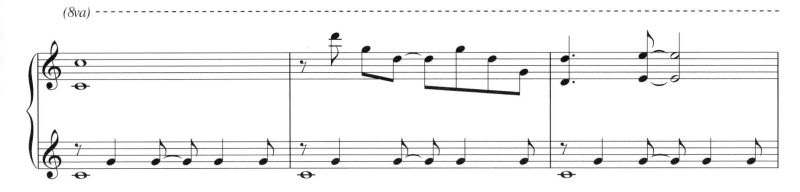

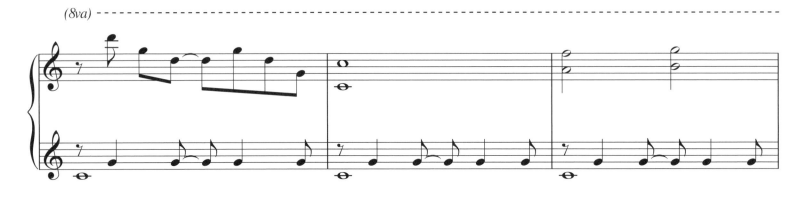

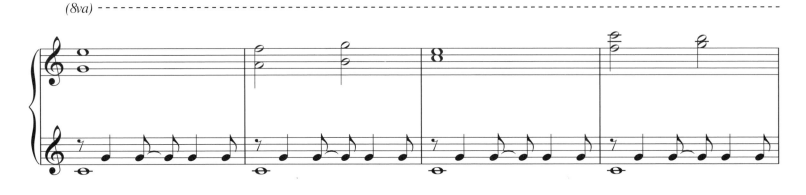

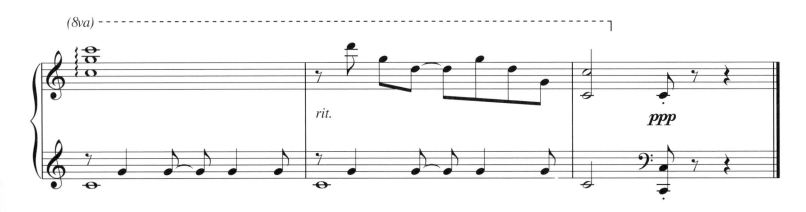

GOLDEN SLUMBERS

Words and Music by JOHN LENNON
and PAUL McCARTNEY

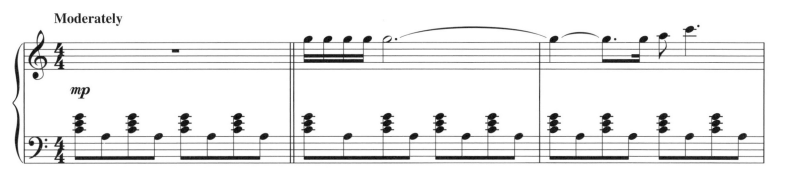

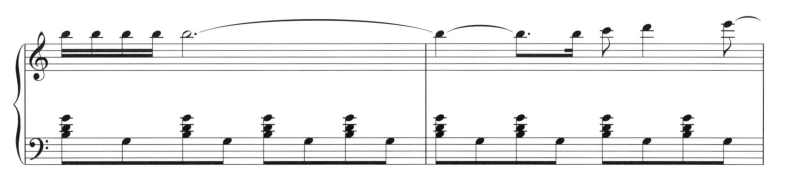

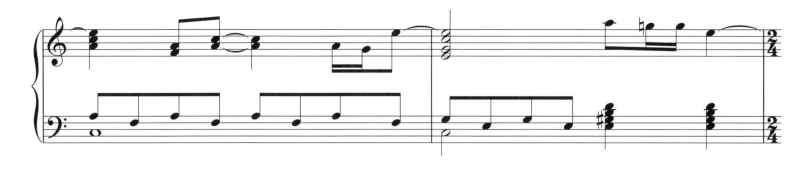

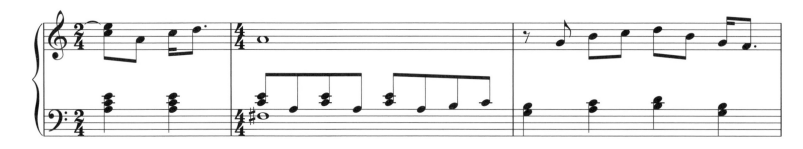

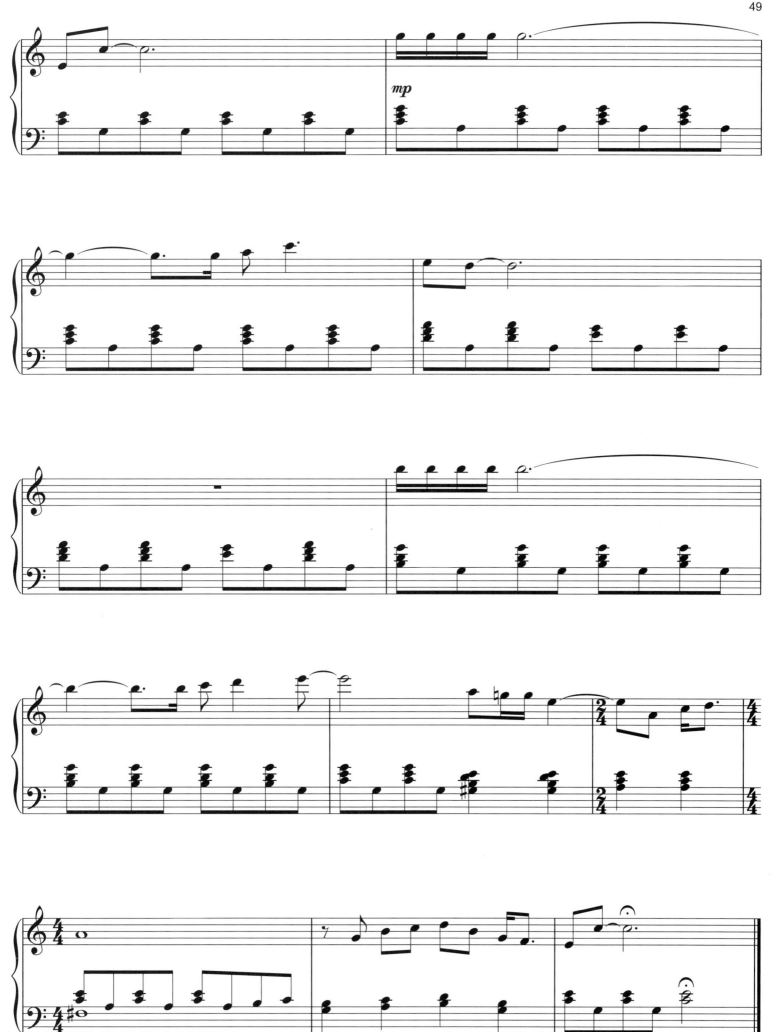

GOD BLESS THE U.S.A.

Words and Music by
LEE GREENWOOD

Slowly

D.S. al Coda

GRENADE

Words and Music by BRUNO MARS,
ARI LEVINE, PHILIP LAWRENCE,
CHRISTOPHER STEVEN BROWN, CLAUDE KELLY
and ANDREW WYATT

Moderately fast

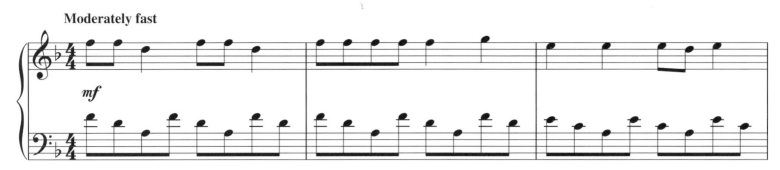

To Coda ⊕

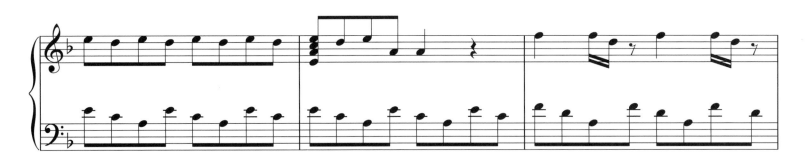

D.S. al Coda

HALLELUJAH

Words and Music by
LEONARD COHEN

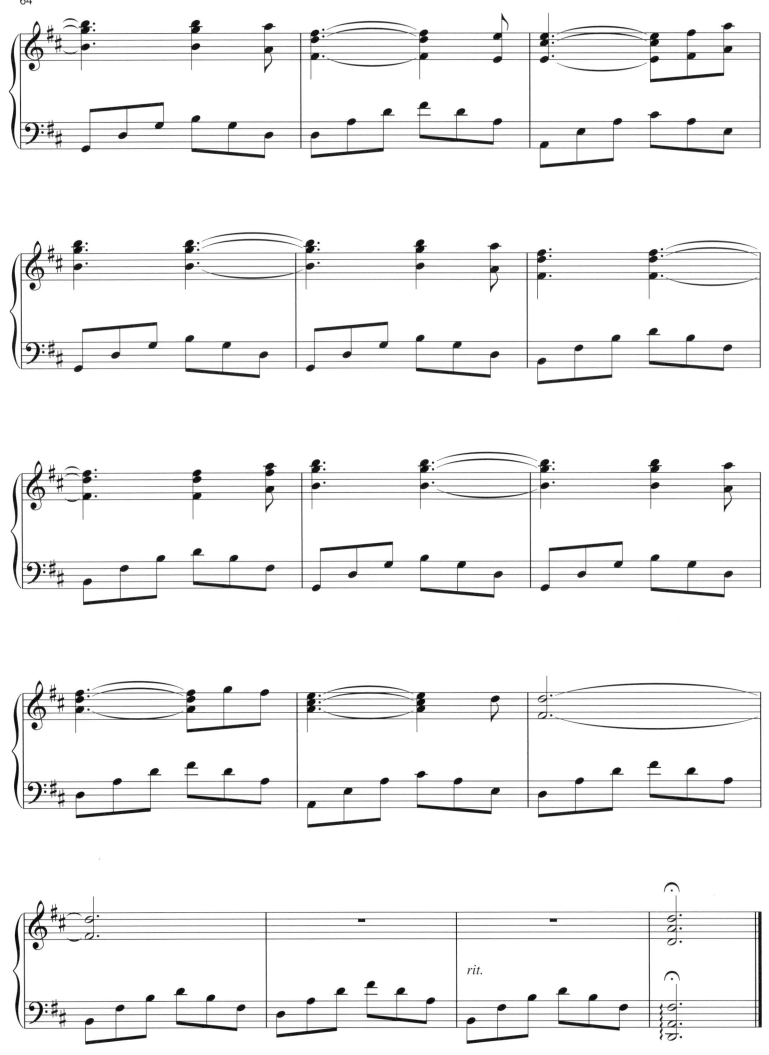

HEART AND SOUL
from the Paramount Short Subject A SONG IS BORN

Words by FRANK LOESSER
Music by HOAGY CARMICHAEL

HELLO

Words and Music by
LIONEL RICHIE

Slow Ballad

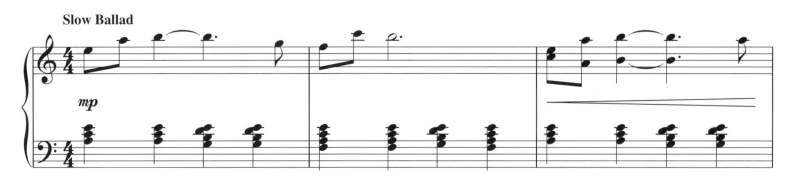

HIDDEN AWAY

Words and Music by JOSH GROBAN
and DAN WILSON

Moderately slow

JUST THE WAY YOU ARE

Words and Music by
BILLY JOEL

I WILL

Words and Music by JOHN LENNON
and PAUL McCARTNEY

JUST THE WAY YOU ARE

Words and Music by BRUNO MARS,
ARI LEVINE, PHILIP LAWRENCE,
KHARI CAIN and KHALIL WALTON

Moderate Hip-Hop groove

CODA

LET IT BE

Words and Music by JOHN LENNON
and PAUL McCARTNEY

THE PINK PANTHER

from THE PINK PANTHER

By HENRY MANCINI

ON MY OWN
from LES MISÉRABLES

Music by CLAUDE-MICHEL SCHÖNBERG
Lyrics by ALAIN BOUBLIL, JEAN-MARC NATEL,
HERBERT KRETZMER, JOHN CAIRD and TREVOR NUNN

Very slowly, but steadily

SOMEONE LIKE YOU

Words and Music by ADELE ADKINS
and DAN WILSON

Moderate Piano Ballad

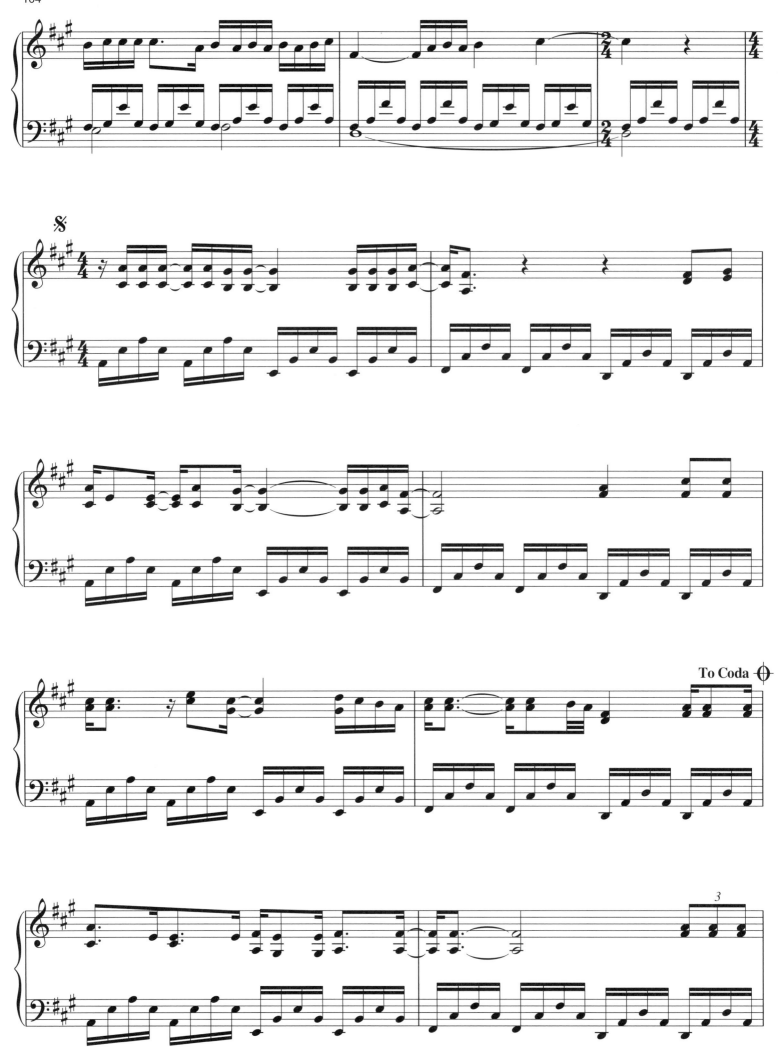

D.S. al Coda

CODA

SPARTACUS – LOVE THEME

from the Universal-International Picture Release SPARTACUS

By ALEX NORTH

TIME TO SAY GOODBYE

Words and Music by LUCIO QUARANTOTTO
and FRANCESCO SARTONI
English translation by FRANK PETERSON

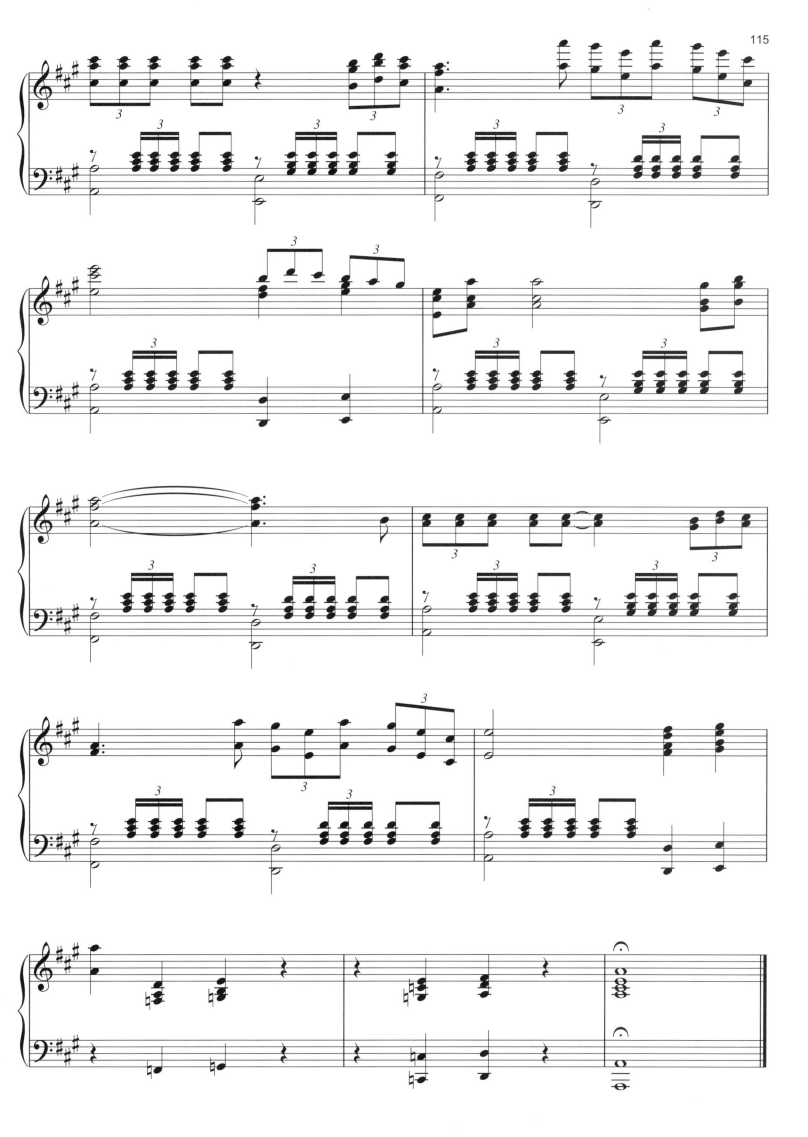

WHEN SHE LOVED ME

from Walt Disney Pictures' TOY STORY 2 - A Pixar Film

Music and Lyrics by
RANDY NEWMAN

WHITE HORSE

Words and Music by TAYLOR SWIFT
and LIZ ROSE

YOUR FAVORITE MUSIC
ARRANGED FOR PIANO SOLO

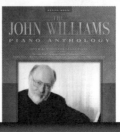

ARTIST, COMPOSER, TV & MOVIE SONGBOOKS

**Adele for Piano Solo –
3rd Edition**
00820186 .... $19.99

The Beatles Piano Solo
00294023 .... $17.99

**A Charlie Brown
Christmas**
00313176 .... $17.99

**Paul Cardall –
The Hymns Collection**
00295925 .... $24.99

Coldplay for Piano Solo
00307637 .... $17.99

**Selections from
Final Fantasy**
00148699 .... $19.99

**Alexis Ffrench – The
Sheet Music Collection**
00345258 .... $19.99

Game of Thrones
00199166 .... $19.99

Hamilton
00354612 .... $19.99

**Hillsong Worship
Favorites**
00303164 .... $14.99

How to Train Your Dragon
00138210 .... $22.99

Elton John Collection
00306040 .... $24.99

La La Land
00283691 .... $14.99

John Legend Collection
00233195 .... $17.99

Les Misérables
00290271 .... $19.99

Little Women
00338470 .... $19.99

Outlander: The Series
00254460 .... $19.99

**The Peanuts®
Illustrated Songbook**
00313178 .... $29.99

**Astor Piazzolla –
Piano Collection**
00285510 .... $19.99

**Pirates of the Caribbean -
Curse of the Black Pearl**
00313256 .... $19.99

Pride & Prejudice
00123854 .... $17.99

Queen
00289784 .... $19.99

John Williams Anthology
00194555 .... $24.99

George Winston Piano Solos
00306822 .... $22.99

MIXED COLLECTIONS

**Beautiful Piano
Instrumentals**
00149926 .... $16.99

**Best Jazz
Piano Solos Ever**
00312079 .... $24.99

Best Piano Solos Ever
00242928 .... $22.99

**Big Book of
Classical Music**
00310508 .... $24.99

Big Book of Ragtime Piano
00311749 .... $22.99

*Prices, content, and availability subject
to change without notice.*

Christmas Medleys
00350572 .... $16.99

Disney Medleys
00242588 .... $19.99

Disney Piano Solos
00313128 .... $17.99

Favorite Pop Piano Solos
00312523 .... $16.99

Great Piano Solos
00311273 .... $19.99

**The Greatest Video
Game Music**
00201767 .... $19.99

Disney characters and artwork TM & © 2021 Disney

Most Relaxing Songs
00233879 .... $17.99

**Movie Themes
Budget Book**
00289137 .... $14.99

**100 of the Most Beautiful
Piano Solos Ever**
00102787 .... $29.99

100 Movie Songs
00102804 .... $29.99

Peaceful Piano Solos
00286009 .... $17.99

**Piano Solos for
All Occasions**
00310964 .... $24.99

**River Flows in You &
Other Eloquent Songs**
00123854 .... $17.99

Sunday Solos for Piano
00311272 .... $17.99

Top Hits for Piano Solo
00294635 .... $14.99

HAL•LEONARD®

View songlists online and order from your
favorite music retailer at
halleonard.com

THE ULTIMATE SONGBOOKS

Hal•Leonard®
PIANO PLAY-ALONG

These great songbook/audio packs come with our standard arrangements for piano and voice with guitar chord frames plus audio. The audio includes a full performance of each song, as well as a second track without the piano part so you can play "lead" with the band!

BOOK/CD PACKS

No.	Title	Cat.	Price
1.	Movie Music	00311072	$14.95
7.	Love Songs	00311078	$14.95
12.	Christmas Favorites	00311137	$15.95
15.	Favorite Standards	00311146	$14.95
27.	Andrew Lloyd Webber Greats	00311179	$14.95
28.	Lennon & McCartney	00311180	$14.95
44.	Frank Sinatra – Popular Hits	00311277	$14.95
71.	George Gershwin	00102687	$24.99
77.	Elton John Favorites	00311884	$14.99
78.	Eric Clapton	00311885	$14.99
81.	Josh Groban	00311901	$14.99
82.	Lionel Richie	00311902	$14.99
86.	Barry Manilow	00311935	$14.99
87.	Patsy Cline	00311936	$14.99
90.	Irish Favorites	00311969	$14.99
92.	Disney Favorites	00311973	$14.99
97.	Great Classical Themes	00312020	$14.99
98.	Christmas Cheer	00312021	$14.99
105.	Bee Gees	00312055	$14.99
106.	Carole King	00312056	$14.99
107.	Bob Dylan	00312057	$16.99
108.	Simon & Garfunkel	00312058	$16.99
114.	Motown	00312176	$14.99
115.	John Denver	00312249	$14.99
123.	Chris Tomlin	00312563	$14.99
125.	Katy Perry	00109373	$14.99

BOOKS/ONLINE AUDIO

No.	Title	Cat.	Price
5.	Disney	00311076	$14.99
8.	The Piano Guys – Uncharted	00202549	$24.99
9.	The Piano Guys – Christmas Together	00259567	$24.99
16.	Coldplay	00316506	$17.99
20.	La La Land	00241591	$19.99
24.	Les Misérables	00311169	$14.99
25.	The Sound of Music	00311175	$15.99
30.	Elton John Hits	00311182	$17.99
31.	Carpenters	00311183	$17.99
32.	Adele	00156222	$24.99
33.	Peanuts™	00311227	$17.99
34.	A Charlie Brown Christmas	00311228	$16.99
46.	Wicked	00311317	$17.99
62.	Billy Joel Hits	00311465	$14.99
65.	Casting Crowns	00311494	$14.99
69.	Pirates of the Caribbean	00311807	$17.99
72.	Van Morrison	00103053	$16.99
73.	Mamma Mia! – The Movie	00311831	$17.99
76.	Pride & Prejudice	00311862	$15.99
83.	Phantom of the Opera	00311903	$16.99
113.	Queen	00312164	$16.99
117.	Alicia Keys	00312306	$17.99
126.	Bruno Mars	00123121	$19.99
127.	Star Wars	00110282	$16.99
128.	Frozen	00126480	$16.99
130.	West Side Story	00130738	$14.99
131.	The Piano Guys – Wonders	00141503 (Contains backing tracks only)	$24.99

HAL•LEONARD®

7777 W. Bluemound Rd. P.O. Box 13819 Milwaukee, WI 53213

Order online from your favorite music retailer at
halleonard.com

Prices, contents and availability subject to change without notice.

PLAY PIANO LIKE A PRO!

AMAZING PHRASING – KEYBOARD
50 Ways to Improve Your Improvisational Skills
by Debbie Denke

Amazing Phrasing is for any keyboard player interested in learning how to improvise and how to improve their creative phrasing. This method is divided into three parts: melody, harmony, and rhythm & style. The online audio contains 44 full-band demos for listening, as well as many play-along examples so you can practice improvising over various musical styles and progressions.
00842030 Book/Online Audio.. $16.99

BEBOP LICKS FOR PIANO
A Dictionary of Melodic Ideas for Improvisation
by Les Wise

Written for the musician who is interested in acquiring a firm foundation for playing jazz, this unique book/audio pack presents over 800 licks. By building up a vocabulary of these licks, players can connect them together in endless possibilities to form larger phrases and complete solos. The book includes piano notation, and the online audio contains helpful note-for-note demos of every lick.
00311854 Book/Online Audio... $17.99

BOOGIE WOOGIE FOR BEGINNERS
by Frank Paparelli

A short easy method for learning to play boogie woogie, designed for the beginner and average pianist. Includes: exercises for developing left-hand bass • 25 popular boogie woogie bass patterns • arrangements of "Down the Road a Piece" and "Answer to the Prayer" by well-known pianists • a glossary of musical terms for dynamics, tempo and style.
00120517 .... $10.99

HAL LEONARD JAZZ PIANO METHOD
by Mark Davis

This is a comprehensive and easy-to-use guide designed for anyone interested in playing jazz piano – from the complete novice just learning the basics to the more advanced player who wishes to enhance their keyboard vocabulary. The accompanying audio includes demonstrations of all the examples in the book! Topics include essential theory, chords and voicings, improvisation ideas, structure and forms, scales and modes, rhythm basics, interpreting a lead sheet, playing solos, and much more!
00131102 Book/Online Audio... $19.99

INTROS, ENDINGS & TURNAROUNDS FOR KEYBOARD
Essential Phrases for Swing, Latin, Jazz Waltz, and Blues Styles
by John Valerio

Learn the intros, endings and turnarounds that all of the pros know and use! This new keyboard instruction book by John Valerio covers swing styles, ballads, Latin tunes, jazz waltzes, blues, major and minor keys, vamps and pedal tones, and more.
00290525 .... $12.99

JAZZ PIANO TECHNIQUE
Exercises, Etudes & Ideas for Building Chops
by John Valerio

This one-of-a-kind book applies traditional technique exercises to specific jazz piano needs. Topics include: scales (major, minor, chromatic, pentatonic, etc.), arpeggios (triads, seventh chords, upper structures), finger independence exercises (static position, held notes, Hanon exercises), parallel interval scales and exercises (thirds, fourths, tritones, fifths, sixths, octaves), and more! The online audio includes 45 recorded examples.
00312059 Book/Online Audio... $19.99

JAZZ PIANO VOICINGS
An Essential Resource for Aspiring Jazz Musicians
by Rob Mullins

The jazz idiom can often appear mysterious and difficult for musicians who were trained to play other types of music. Long-time performer and educator Rob Mullins helps players enter the jazz world by providing voicings that will help the player develop skills in the jazz genre and start sounding professional right away — without years of study! Includes a "Numeric Voicing Chart," chord indexes in all 12 keys, info about what range of the instrument you can play chords in, and a beginning approach to bass lines.
00310914 .... $19.99

OSCAR PETERSON – JAZZ EXERCISES, MINUETS, ETUDES & PIECES FOR PIANO

Legendary jazz pianist Oscar Peterson has long been devoted to the education of piano students. In this book he offers dozens of pieces designed to empower the student, whether novice or classically trained, with the technique needed to become an accomplished jazz pianist.
00311225 .... $14.99

PIANO AEROBICS
by Wayne Hawkins

Piano Aerobics is a set of exercises that introduces students to many popular styles of music, including jazz, salsa, swing, rock, blues, new age, gospel, stride, and bossa nova. In addition, there is a online audio with accompaniment tracks featuring professional musicians playing in those styles.
00311863 Book/Online Audio $19.99

PIANO FITNESS
A Complete Workout
by Mark Harrison

This book will give you a thorough technical workout, while having fun at the same time! The accompanying online audio allows you to play along with a rhythm section as you practice your scales, arpeggios, and chords in all keys. Instead of avoiding technique exercises because they seem too tedious or difficult, you'll look forward to playing them. Various voicings and rhythmic settings, which are extremely useful in a variety of pop and jazz styles, are also introduced.
00311995 Book/Online Audio... $19.99

HAL•LEONARD®
7777 W. BLUEMOUND RD. P.O. BOX 13819
MILWAUKEE, WISCONSIN 53213

www.halleonard.com

Prices, contents, and availability subject to change without notice.